"…But man, proud man,
Drest in a little brief authority,
Most ignorant of what he's most assur'd,
His glassy essence, like an angry ape,
Plays such fantastic tricks before high heaven,
As make the angels weep…"

William Shakespeare, *Measure for Measure*

Hard Rain

Mark Edwards
Lloyd Timberlake

Lyric by Bob Dylan

Still
Pictures
**Moving
Words**
Defining the
21st Century

First published in Great Britain in 2006 by
Still Pictures Moving Words Ltd
199 Shooters Hill Road
London SE3 8UL, UK

10 9 8 7 6 5 4 3 2 1

A catalogue record for this book is available from the British Library

ISBN-13: 978-1-905588-00-8   ISBN-10: 1-905588-00-3

Design by Mike Kenny
Text editor Mark Reynolds
Printed by Beacon Press, Uckfield

This book is dedicated to my incandescent god-daughter
Alice Jacoby, who will be forever young in these pages.

Contents

World gone wrong

Mark Edwards

It's 9.32 am, July 20, 1969: Apollo 11 mission to the moon. One of the crew – it's not recorded whether it was Armstrong, Aldrin, or Collins – points the Hasselblad camera through the observation window of Command Module Columbia as the earth appears to rise above the rim of the moon, and presses the button.

The photograph the astronaut takes has been seen by almost everyone who has lived since that moment. The image is beautiful, and its effect when it was published was, and has remained, overwhelming. The conspicuous contrast between our living planet and its lifeless moon is buried deep in our collective consciousness.

Human activities on earth do not show up at this distance. Yet this picture is dramatic, irrefutable evidence of our immense and ever-accelerating technological development. Earthrise shows us just how fragile and isolated our civilization really is, and it marks the beginning of the contemporary environmental movement.

While these great events unfolded, I was lost in a lunar landscape myself: the southern edge of the Sahara Desert. I was rescued by a

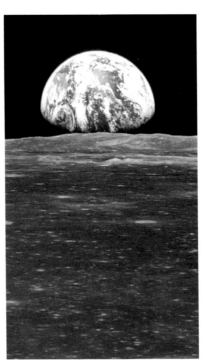

Earthrise. A view of the earth appears over the lunar horizon as the Apollo 11 Command Module nears the Moon. © NASA/Kennedy Space Center.

Tuareg nomad on a camel, in a scene that felt like the opening moments of David Lean's *Lawrence of Arabia*.

He took me to his companions, sat me down on a rock, and went into his hut. He reappeared with an umbrella, a cassette player, and two pieces of wood. He rubbed the sticks together and made a fire. We boiled a pot of water, and we had a nice cup of tea. He warmed the batteries and turned on the cassette player. Bob Dylan sang "A Hard Rain's A-Gonna Fall". I am suddenly in the front row of an extraordinary Dylan concert. I could feel the words – the whole song – taking root in me. He sounded like he was singing to an empty world. I'm surrounded by dignified, graceful people from another age sitting by a fire lit by friction – our first step on the road to becoming an industrial, scientific society. I am looking at the moon as it rises above the edge of the desert. Armstrong and Aldrin are planting an American flag in a lunar crater, their remarkable and extravagant journey made possible by harnessing the explosive power of fire.

Dylan is piling image upon image. The cumulative effect of those images of dead

"If a way to the Better there be, it exacts a full look at the Worst." Thomas Hardy

and dying life is overwhelming. He wrote "Hard Rain" during the Cuban Missile Crisis. The world went to bed one night in 1962 not knowing if it would wake up the next day. But, as Dylan has said, this extraordinary song is open to much wider interpretation: "it doesn't really matter where a song comes from. It just matters where it takes you." We now know that it is not only nuclear war that might bring about our downfall. Our headlong collision with nature makes us dangerous passengers on planet earth. Climate change alone has the potential to be catastrophic. The technology to wipe out civilization is widely available – not everyone can afford it, but the price is coming down. Cheap transport and consumer goods, warm homes, light at the touch of a switch, clean hot and cold water, are available to more and more people in the modern and modernizing world. And it is mostly powered by fossil fuels. The coal, oil, and gas that drive the modern world contain the carbon that plants inhaled hundreds of millions of years ago. We are returning it to the atmosphere through exhaust pipes and smokestacks; it combines with the carbon released from forests when they are burned to create more

agricultural land in poorer countries with rapidly growing populations.

So much of what we do adds carbon dioxide to the atmosphere – eight billion tons each year – and this pollution is changing the climate. There is more heat-trapping carbon dioxide and methane in the atmosphere today than for 55 million years, enough to melt all the ice on the planet, submerge many of the world's principal cities and flood large areas of productive land. A one-metre rise in sea level would displace 20 million people in Bangladesh and India alone. By the middle of the century, man-made warming could trigger irreversible melting of the Greenland ice cap – increasing sea levels by seven metres. We would have to continually redraw the map of the world as coastlines eroded and many of the world's major cities built near the sea became inundated and damaged by storm surges generated by climate instability.

So much that we saw as steps towards a better life has proved to be steps towards ecological disaster. We are turning back the evolutionary clock, recreating the warmer, less stable atmosphere that existed millions of years ago. Our cultural achievements and

Threatened people, threatened species. Yanomami mother breastfeeding her child and a baby monkey in the Orinoco River Basin, Venezuela. Indigenous people are threatened by the destruction of their ancestral lands being cleared to grow crops to expand agricultural land to feed rapidly growing populations.

our mastery of science have made us forget that "human" is just a word for a species of animal, that we are part of nature and dependent on nature. If the climate changes, all of nature changes.

We still do not really believe we are changing the climate. We feel so small, and the sky seems so big; how could anything we do affect the climate? We are in collective denial, sleepwalking blindly towards a tipping point where bigger and deadlier environmental problems overtake our ability to solve them. But the consensus among scientists that man-made climate change is happening now is overwhelming. Of course all the independent scientists could be wrong and the lobbyists, many funded by US oil companies, could be right. And the earth could be flat.

The morning after I listened to "Hard Rain", I noticed that the rock I had been sitting on was actually part of a fossilized tree trunk. I was in the middle of a vast, ancient forest. Five times in the past half-billion years, the fossil record shows us, living things have been wiped out over much of the earth. Climate change, perhaps triggered by the impact of an asteroid, is the likely cause of the

Flooded street, Wertheim, Germany. In the coming century, global sea levels are predicted to rise by up to a metre, threatening regions at or below sea level such as Pacific islands, much of Bangladesh, New Orleans, the Nile Delta, the Netherlands, East Anglia, the Thames Estuary, and river basins throughout the world. The population of Bangladesh will double as its land surface halves. © Peter Frischmuth/Argus/Still Pictures.

"In the Stone Age the ordinary practical intelligence was good enough. People then had an instinctive sort of intelligence developed by culture. But today we have created a complex world. To deal with nature we need a certain kind of intelligence, but to deal with the world thought has created requires a much higher kind of intelligence." David Bohm, *Changing Consciousness*

The electric-powered Lunar Roving Vehicle, or "Moon Buggy", used by the crew of Apollo 15 in 1971. Too little progress has since been made to develop cars powered by fuels that do not generate carbon emissions. © NASA Headquarters/GRIN.

Scrapped bicycle in a lake, Germany. Using bicycles instead of cars is an easy and effective way of reducing our carbon footprint. © Thomas Wolke/UNEP/Still Pictures.

five great natural extinctions that geologists and paleobiologists have identified. These acts of nature, like the 2004 tsunami that ravaged much of Southeast Asia and Hurricane Katrina that devastated New Orleans in 2005, are part of the cycle of life and death that has defined the planet since the beginning of time. We now face the sixth great extinction,

and it will be an entirely human achievement. The combined effects of climate change, acidification of the seas as they soak up atmospheric carbon dioxide, the widespread destruction of forests, wetlands and other natural habitats, are together causing the loss of an estimated 50,000 species a year – an unseen holocaust of biodiversity.

Bob Dylan again. I just made coffee and turned on the radio. It's a BBC programme, *Desert Island Discs*. Each week a celebrity is invited to choose the eight records he or she would take if cast away on a desert island. Today's guest is a man with a quiet, warm, restrained voice, and he's saying he could have chosen eight Bob Dylan records for his island. Sue Lawley, the presenter, plays "Just Like A Woman", then asks her guest about climate change.

He turns out to be Professor Sir David King, the UK government's chief scientific advisor and the man who unexpectedly announced that climate change is the most serious problem facing the world today. He reminds us that the 1990s was the hottest decade on record, and that this was predicted by climate change scientists; that the hot summer of 2003 was the biggest natural disaster in Central Europe, causing an estimated 30,000 people to die prematurely, and that statistical analyses indicate that half the severity of that event could be attributed to climate change. He points out that there will be many impacts as the earth warms.

"But are these facts?" asks Lawley. "Are there scientists who will dispute this, or are you telling us this is irrefutable?"

"The facts are CO_2 levels are 40% higher than any record going back one million years at least. The fact is global temperatures are rising around the world. The fact is we are losing ice from land masses around the world. All of these are facts. In terms of future

Coal-burning power station, Calcutta, India. Rapidly developing countries need access to technology that traps CO_2 for safe storage underground. The modern world needs to set an example and fit all fossil fuel-powered stations with CO_2-trapping technology.

"For everything that makes Africa hard to inhabit today will be made harder by global warming. Hunger will be made more acute; shortage of clean water will be more degrading; disease will be more painful, crippling and deadly; natural disasters will be more overwhelming... Africa can be ruined by the atmosphere as well as by economics." Michael McCarthy, *Independent*

Power-generating solar panels in Waat, Sudan. Governments and industry need to scale up investment in renewable energy systems. © Hartmut Schwarzbach/Argus/Still Pictures.

impacts, there is an enormous amount of discussion. But the science is telling us what the risks are. The technologies that are being developed are going to be there to deal with the problem. The final question is: is there the political will around the world to actually invest in this technology?"

Governments need to lead and they need to be led. The cancellation of the debts of the world's poorest countries in 2005 was a stunning triumph for the mass movement of concerned individuals and UK Chancellor of the Exchequer Gordon Brown who brokered the deal. But without corresponding action to halt climate change, people in those countries will be plunged into even more desperate straits. And children alive now in the modern and modernizing world will grow up in an increasingly insecure environment as our society slides back into poverty. Climate change is handcuffed to poverty. If we don't start cooling the planet your children's families will be impoverished, culture will be impoverished and nature will be impoverished.

Global cooling doesn't attract much support from the world of celebrities.

Don't expect huge concerts with pop stars demanding the audience insulate their homes, buy food at the nearest farmers' market, travel by bike and public transport whenever possible and stop wasting energy. It doesn't rhyme. But if we care about poverty and nature and future generations that's what we have to do for starters. Actually the new low-carbon culture is not bad. Food from farmers' markets tastes better, cycling feels great and insulation means your home will be warmed at a lower cost and will stay cooler in summer. Planting trees to absorb the carbon you produce in this changeover period is not the perfect solution, but if you can afford to fly to foreign countries for holidays you can afford to pay your own carbon tax.

What is needed now is a "majority movement" to support a range of practical measures that will reduce our dependency on fossil fuels. Humanity will have to put aside the deep divisions it has maintained for thousands and thousands of years and take practical steps to solve this problem. The prize will be to deflect military spending, currently one trillion dollars of global taxpayers' money a year, to pay to reinvent the modern world so that it

A bulldozer abandoned during an uncompleted road-building project, Burkina Faso; a monument to inappropriate aid.

is compatible with nature. This would require a coalition of those in the peace movement, environmentalists, those who support the campaign against poverty – and the silent majority. They have to find their voice. Unless they do, a hard rain's a-gonna fall.

There have been many mass movements, relatively small groups of people campaigning on a wide range of issues, but humanity has never acted collectively. Nothing less will do. If we are to solve our problems we need a new spirit of human co-operation. There is a lovely Buddhist story that illustrates this point better than 1,000 photographs. There was a bush covered in fruit that attracted a lot of birds. They were regularly caught by a birdcatcher throwing a net over them. Other birds seeing this said, "Look, if we all flew up together at the same time we could lift the net up and escape." So they did this and all went well until one day one of the birds complained he was putting in more effort than the rest. They all began to argue and while they were still arguing the birdcatcher caught them all.

Environmental destruction and poverty are problems affecting a deeply divided world. As we have seen, it costs a trillion dollars a year

Children protest against traffic pollution, Turin, Italy. © Angelo Doto/UNEP/Still Pictures.

to defend the national boundaries the human race created.

The finger-pointing protest movement of the 60s may have had its place, but this time round the finger points at all of us in the modern world: individuals, governments and companies. We will all have to take a lot of small steps. We have become used to wasting energy; our homes and cities leak heat and light. Governments will have to work together and take a "giant leap for mankind", not just act in the interests of their own constituency. They have to set the agenda that will transform our outdated carbon-polluting technology and develop new transport systems, new technologies to generate electricity without carbon emissions, and an internationally agreed legal framework for businesses, so they can plan for the future knowing their investments in low-carbon technologies will be worthwhile.

The climate crisis is a problem so huge, complicated and fundamentally implicated in Western lifestyles that most politicians see little to be gained from engaging with it at all. But global warming is a more serious threat to democracy than the Cold War and a much more difficult problem to solve. You knew where the enemy was during the Cold War. Now we are the enemy. If civilization is severely damaged by an environmental cataclysm, democracy will be an early victim, as societies revert to the survival of the fittest. (New Orleans' rapid collapse into anarchy after the devastation caused by Hurricane Katrina was a vivid reminder of what can happen to a city in the richest country on earth.) Elected politicians are prepared to go to great lengths to install and support new democratic governments in countries around the world, but do little to deal with this real threat to world security. The atomic bomb may not be used again, but man-made climate change is happening now. Humankind is unleashing a phenomenon whose nature, scale, and consequences are unprecedented.

Problems, however severe, present many opportunities. If climate change is to be checked, scientists will have to create new low-carbon technologies, but many who could play a key role are funded by governments to invent weapons of mass destruction for the military, or are employed by industry to research and develop new consumer goods.

Migrant family, India. There are about a billion squatters in the world today – one in every six humans on the planet. Every day, close to two hundred thousand people leave their ancestral homes in rural regions and move to the cities. Almost a million and a half people a week, or seventy million a year. Within 25 years, the number of squatters is expected to double.

When leading business figures are asked what they see as the most pressing problem facing business in the future, they agree that it is climate change. You would imagine that the captains of industry would want to prove that capitalism plus technology can address our problems. Some do, and these are the companies to support and invest in. But most only pay lip service to the problem; they cut down on waste, but they don't cut down on double-talk. The CEO of one of the world's biggest car manufacturers makes impressive speeches about sustainability while his company engages in a battle to sell us more environmentally destructive SUVs.

While some business leaders are slowly responding to climate change, religious leaders have hardly acknowledged the problem. They have a record of concern for people living in poverty, but not for an issue that is likely to disproportionately harm vulnerable people in poor countries and lead to migrations on a biblical scale, resulting in uncountable deaths.

Philanthropists and foundations currently provide very little support to help solve the climate crisis. As an issue, climate change received just over a third of 1% of all US

"If you want to compare it (the debate over the existence of global warming) to a football match, it is more like Manchester United taking on three primary school children... On one hand, you have the entire scientific community and on the other a handful of people, half of them crackpots. Nevertheless, this is still presented as an unresolved battle. This is simply not true. It has been resolved. Only the details of climate change's impact have still to be worked out." Lord May of Oxford, former President of the Royal Society

Children collecting water from the village pump, Silmiougou, Burkina Faso. This pump is operable for six months a year. The rest of the time women have to walk three kilometres to collect water.

foundation grants in 2000. The positive achievements of their funding are likely to be overwhelmed by climate change.

History is partly a record of fallen civilizations. Most societies that have perished have done so through neglect and self-delusion; they have failed to rise to the challenges they faced. If we care about the world, about people living in miserable poverty now and about future generations, we should be mobilizing resources to develop sustainable technologies with the single-minded determination seen when countries prepare for world war. The Cuban Missile Crisis reminded us not only that individuals are mortal, but that society itself is mortal, that choosing well or badly among policies and possibilities determines what becomes of us.

On the heath, Lear asks Gloucester how he sees the world. Gloucester, who is blind, answers: "I see it feelingly." Why don't we feel the world enough to save it? What prevents us from collaborating in a global effort to solve the climate crisis? Is it because the consequences are unimaginable? If so, we need artists of every discipline to use their skills to cast light on our failure of perception

Polar Bears, Hudson Bay, Canada. The world's largest carnivores, a symbol of the Arctic, may be the first spectacular casualty of global warming as the ice shelves on which they depend to hunt seals are rapidly melting and may be gone by mid-century. Some scientists believe human civilization is bringing about the sixth great extinction. © Thomas D. Mangelsen/Peter Arnold Inc/Still Pictures.

Great White Shark caught in a deep-water driftnet, Santa Barbara, USA. Perhaps the most devastating means of fishing in the world, walls of death created by driftnets indiscriminately kill everything in their path. © Tom Campbell/UNEP/Still Pictures.

and bring the uncertain future alive in our imaginations. Only symbolic language can bear the strain of a threat on the scale posed by climate change.

The expression "a snowball's chance in hell" comes to mind when you consider the likelihood of human beings working together to reverse global warming and making poverty – not just African poverty – history. Like all great projects it requires a large measure of tactical optimism. It may already be too late to halt global warming. It may be too difficult or too expensive, but life for me is made more interesting by responding to the challenge, of both the "*in*vironmental" crisis which has produced a world where human beings are deeply divided by nationalism and sectarian beliefs, and the environmental crisis.

I had the idea to illustrate "Hard Rain" as I listened to Dylan in the desert. In an interview in 1965 he said, "The words came fast – very fast... Line after line, trying to capture the feeling of nothingness." Well, the pictures came slowly. What made this photo essay possible, at least in the beginning before I got assignments, was a discovery a friend and I made one evening. We realized that no one ever checked air tickets as you leave an airplane. All we had to do to fly a long way from London was buy a cheap ticket to the first destination, usually Paris or Amsterdam. When the plane landed, we waited until all the new passengers were on board, and we took an empty seat. We got off a lot further away: New Delhi, Bangkok, Nairobi. Bootleg travel: it was wrong, and all I can say in mitigation is that it provided the environmental movement with some fundraising images it might not have otherwise had. (Don't try it now. Since the first hijacking, airlines check the passengers at each stop.)

I feel bad about stowing away on jumbo jets; I feel worse about the CO_2 pollution I'm responsible for, but I used the opportunity those trips gave me to photograph people trying to exist at the sharp end of the environmental debate. I never knew when a line of "Hard Rain" would appear before me: a man carrying his wife to safety during a flood in Bangladesh, my god-daughter surrounded by bubbles showing me how high she could jump on her trampoline, a man whose family was too poor to cremate him being eaten by dogs behind the Taj Mahal.

Dylan's instinctive awareness of the capacities of symbolic language in "Hard Rain" is turned to brilliant use. He describes "Hard Rain" as "a song of desperation", "a song of terror". This is a book of desperation. I have seen Dylan's words in the viewfinder of my camera and in photographs taken by my friends. With their help, it should not take quite so much imagination for us to understand the future scientists are predicting.

Turn the pages and see feelingly.

Mark Edwards
London, 2006

A Hard Rain's A-Gonna Fall

Oh, where have you been, my blue-eyed son?
Oh, where have you been, my darling young one?

I've stumbled on the side of twelve misty mountains,

I've walked and I've crawled on six crooked highways,

I've stepped in the middle of seven sad forests,

I've been out in front of a dozen dead oceans,

I've been ten thousand miles
in the mouth of a graveyard,

And it's a hard, and it's a hard,
it's a hard, and it's a hard,
And it's a hard rain's a-gonna fall.

Oh, what did you see, my blue-eyed son?
Oh, what did you see, my darling young one?

I saw a
newborn baby
with wild wolves
all around it,

I saw a highway
of diamonds with nobody on it,

I saw a black branch with blood that kept drippin',

I saw a room full of men with their hammers a-bleedin',

I saw a white ladder
all covered with water,

I saw ten thousand talkers whose tongues were all broken,

I saw guns and sharp swords in the hands of young children,

And it's a hard, and it's a hard,
it's a hard, it's a hard,
And it's a hard rain's a-gonna fall.

And what did you hear, my blue-eyed son?
And what did you hear, my darling young one?

I heard the sound of a thunder, it roared out a warnin',

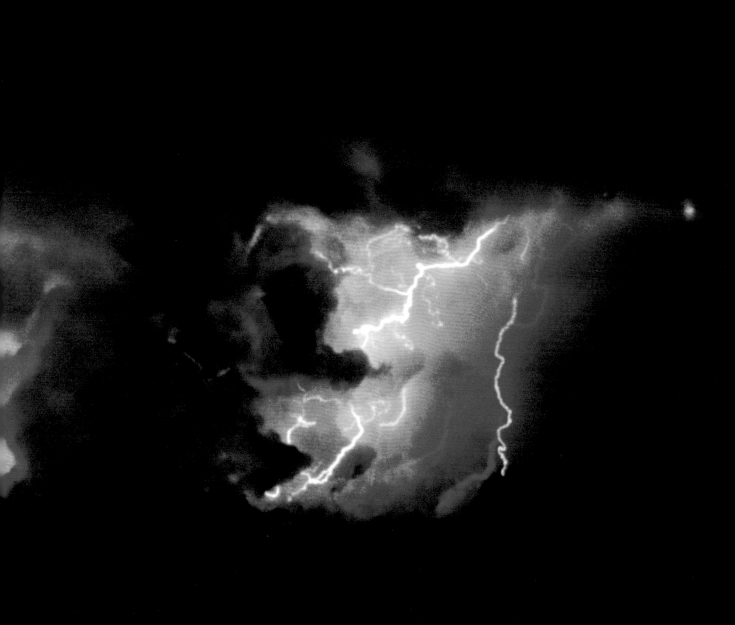

Heard the roar of a wave that could
drown the whole world,

Heard one hundred drummers
whose hands were a-blazin',

Heard ten thousand whisperin'
and nobody listenin',

Heard one person starve,
I heard many people laughin',

Heard the song of a poet who died in the gutter,

Heard the sound
of a clown who
cried in the alley,

And it's a hard, and it's a hard,
it's a hard, it's a hard,
And it's a hard rain's a-gonna fall.

Oh, who did you meet, my blue-eyed son?
Who did you meet, my darling young one?

I met a young child beside a dead pony,

I met a white man who walked a black dog,

I met a young woman
whose body was burning,

I met a young girl, she gave me a rainbow,

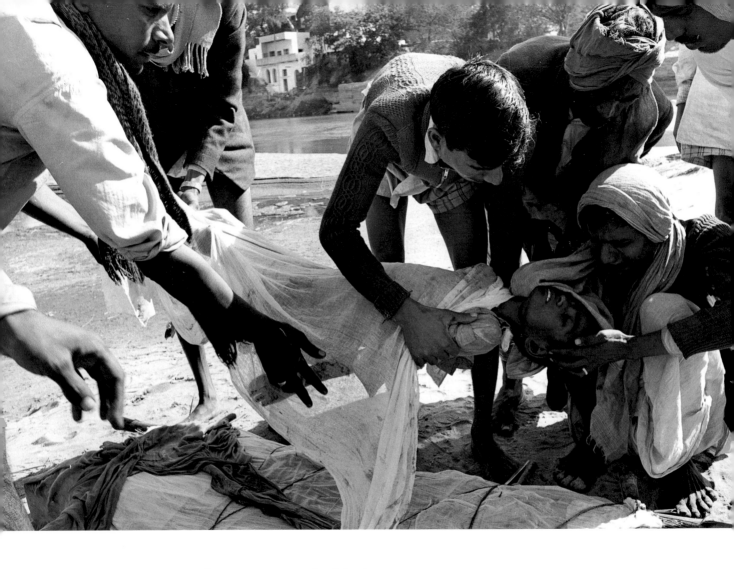

I met one man who was wounded in love,

I met another man who
was wounded with hatred,

And it's a hard, it's a hard,
it's a hard, it's a hard,
It's a hard rain's a-gonna fall.

Oh, what'll you do now, my blue-eyed son?
Oh, what'll you do now, my darling young one?

I'm a-goin' back out 'fore the rain starts a-fallin',

I'll walk to the
depths of the
deepest black forest,

Where the people are many and their hands are all empty,

Where the pellets of poison are flooding their waters,

Where the home in the valley
meets the damp dirty prison,

Where the executioner's face
is always well hidden,

Where hunger is
ugly, where souls
are forgotten,

Where black is the color, where none is the number,

And I'll tell it and think it and speak it and breathe it,

And reflect it from
the mountain so all
souls can see it,

Then I'll stand on the ocean until I start sinkin',
But I'll know my song well before I start singin',

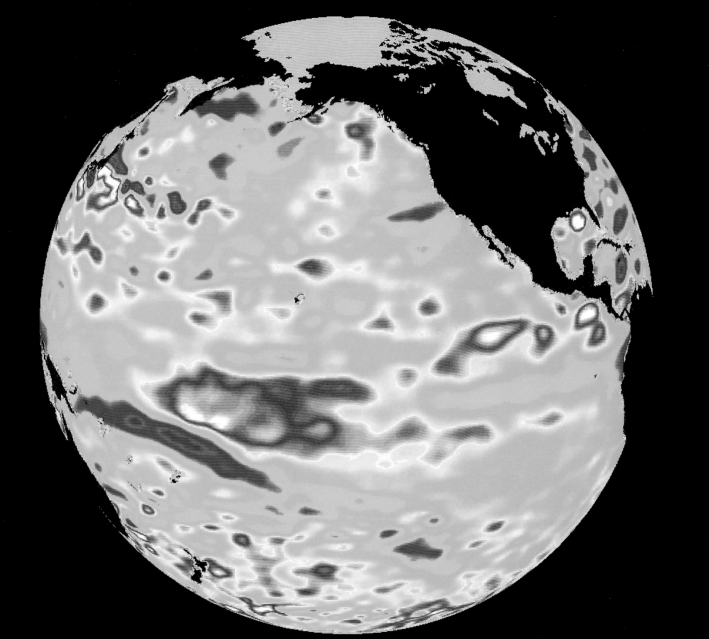

And it's a hard, it's a hard,
it's a hard, it's a hard,
It's a hard rain's a-gonna fall.

Photographs © Mark Edwards/Still Pictures
unless otherwise credited.

Outskirts of Kathmandu, Nepal, Christmas Day 1969.
Today every inch of the landscape is covered with
houses; the mountains cannot be seen through the
smog. Rapidly increasing populations in many parts of
the developing world, environmental degradation and
the demise of rural economies have contributed to a
rapid increase in the number of people living in cities.

Refugees from East Pakistan arriving in India during
the Bangladesh war in 1971. 10 million people crossed
the border during the conflict. A sea level rise of one
metre would displace an estimated 20 million people
in India and Bangladesh.

Haiti today. In a letter to King Ferdinand of Spain in
1493, Christopher Columbus described sighting the
island: "Its lands are high; there are in it many sierras
and very lofty mountains, beyond comparison with
that of Tenerife. All are most beautiful, of a thousand
shapes; all are accessible and are filled with trees of
a thousand kinds and tall, so that they seem to touch
the sky. I am told that they never lose their foliage,
and this I can believe, for I saw them as green and
lovely as they are in Spain in May, and some of them
were flowering, some bearing fruit, and some at
another stage, according to their nature." Some 98%
of Haiti's forests have been cut down since 1960 and
turned into charcoal cooking fuel.

Seabird caught in an oil spill, Brazil.
© D. Rodrigues/UNEP/Still Pictures.

The body of a man whose family is too poor to buy
wood for his cremation lies on a sandbank behind the
Taj Mahal, Agra, India.

Hard rain, Haiti.

A child suffering from malnutrition in a remote
village in Haiti.

A stream of meltwater cascading off the vast Arctic
ice sheet which covers Greenland, now melting
because of global warming.
© Professor R. J. Braithwaite/Still Pictures.

Amazon jungle being burned to expand agricultural
land, Brazil.
© John Maier/Still Pictures.

One of the 4.7 million British cattle suspected of having Bovine Spongiform Encephalopathy (BSE). For 10 years the government told the people that there is no evidence that BSE can be transmitted to humans. In fact, it can be transmitted to people and is a fatal illness.
© Nigel Dickinson/Still Pictures.

Rainy day in the English countryside.

Portraits of political prisoners tortured during the Pol Pot regime. Tuol Sleng prison camp, Cambodia.
© Mike Kolloffel/Still Pictures.

Child with a toy gun, Bucharest, Romania.[1]

Hard rain, Haiti.

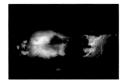

Thunderstorm, Wisconsin, USA.
© Keith Kent/Peter Arnold Inc/Still Pictures.

2004 tsunami, Sri Lanka. A young woman discovers the body of her brother. Tsunamis are an entirely natural phenomenon, but scientists have warned that rising sea levels and extreme weather events will be a consequence of our reckless use of fossil fuels.
© Arko Datta/Reuters.

Voodoo ceremony: devotees appeal to the gods for rain, Haiti.

Feeding centre during the 1985 drought in Ethiopia. Many scientists now believe that the drought that killed hundreds of thousands in the 1970s and 80s in Ethiopia and the Sahel region of Africa, leading to the Band Aid movement, may have been partly caused by Western air pollution from cars and power stations. Burning coal and oil produces tiny airborne particles of soot, ash, sulphur compounds and other pollutants. This visible pollution changes the optical properties of clouds, masking the effects of global warming and interfering with rainfall.
© Chris Steele-Perkins/Magnum.

Central Park, New York, USA.

Homeless man, London, UK.

1 Moments after taking this photograph the military policeman pointing at the camera arrested me. As he did so an elderly man came up to me and repeated the quote from *Measure for Measure* that prefaces this book. – Mark Edwards

Copenhagen carnival, Denmark.

Hard rain, Haiti.

San Bushman boy from Makiri village, Namibia, whose horse is dying due to drought.
© Mark Hakansson/Panos Pictures.

An unmuzzled dog appears to be used to frighten a detainee at Abu Ghraib prison in Iraq, 2004. Two military dog handlers told investigators that intelligence personnel ordered them to use dogs to intimidate prisoners.
Photographer unknown.

Home care for people dying of AIDS, Addis Ababa, Ethiopia. Volunteers, many of whom are HIV positive, provide basic medical care for those too ill to look after themselves.

Alice Jacoby on her trampoline, UK.

Agra, India. A father buries his son, one of the millions of children who die an unnecessary death each year in developing countries.

Shattered graveyard portrait of a dead Palestinian, Lebanon.
© Chris Steele-Perkins/Magnum.

Hard rain, Haiti.

Tropical Rainforest, Canaima National Park, Venezuela.
© David Woodfall/WWI/Still Pictures.

Suri Amazonian children watch a bulldozer cutting a logging road through their reservation, Brazil.

Serra Pelada gold mine, the Amazon, Brazil.
© Sebastião Salgado/NB Pictures.

Children scavenge rubbish from Manila Bay, Philippines. It will be sold through a chain of dealers and eventually recycled.
© Hartmut Schwarzbach/UNEP/Still Pictures.

La Paz, Bolivia.

Copenhagen carnival, Denmark.

An orphaned child suffering from malnutrition waits for treatment in a field hospital during the Bangladesh war, India.

Andromeda Galaxy.
© O. Sauzereau/BIOS/Still Pictures.

Drought in Ethiopia. A woman lies dying at the feet of two photographers and 20 journalists.

Glacier in Jacabamba Valley, Peru, photographed in 1980 by Bryan Lynas (left) and in 2002 by his son.
© Bryan and Mark Lynas/Still Pictures.

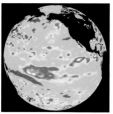

Satellite image showing ocean temperatures. The oceans eventually absorb 84% of the earth's extra heat, and the Atlantic, Indian, and Pacific oceans are all half a degree warmer at the surface than 40 years ago. The distribution of that heat exactly matches what climate models predict would be the effect of warming caused by human activity. Computer models that incorporate only natural causes such as solar or volcanic activity do not explain or match the temperature changes.
© NASA/Jet Propulsion Laboratory.

Hard rain, Haiti.

No shelter

Lloyd Timberlake

Bob Dylan wrote "Hard Rain" during the Cuban crisis. He painted a grim, end-of-the-world picture of an acid, killing rain, the very opposite of Chaucer's *shoures sote* (sweet showers) that pierce the drought and renew the earth. Dylan's rain kills: people, animals, plants and the very fabric of evolution.

As the threat of a superpower nuclear exchange has receded, we have grown careless in our control of nuclear materials and stockpiles of weapons. So nuclear blasts remain a real threat.

However, the truly astonishing thing about Dylan's song of more than 40 years ago is that its lyrics seem to describe in broad, poetic strokes a more complex, intertwined, and multi-pronged planet-rending scenario, one only beginning to be thought about in the early 1960s. It is hard to describe in a few words, but is best summed up as a wilful, inane and immoral carelessness in regard both to people and planet by our leaders and ourselves.

Great, wrenching catastrophes will occur this century, causing unimaginable human suffering and environmental destruction, disrupting human development and natural evolution.

How can I be so sure? Because the suffering and destruction began some time ago.

You hadn't noticed? No. Our failure to notice is one of the main reasons there is no stopping this hard rain.

The naïve observer

I rushed away from my university, skipping my graduation ceremony, straight to a school in Tanzania, East Africa, for members of revolutionary parties in southern Africa: from Angola, Namibia, South Africa, Mozambique, and Zimbabwe. First, I was trying to keep from being drafted and sent to the Vietnam War. Second, I had never been out of the United States, had grown up in the South during the end of the United States' own apartheid system (buses I rode as a boy in Atlanta had signs saying "White passengers will seat from front; coloured passengers will seat from rear."); so the strangest and most romantic place I could think of visiting was Africa. Third, I had a deep desire to be able to say casually in later life that I had "trained African revolutionaries".

I did train them, mainly to read Dickens and Shakespeare, do maths, and raise chickens (my grandfather had a chicken farm). They were good, eager students. Their parties took them away for long periods of time to train them in revolution; so I was free to wander about East Africa, sneak into parts of the Serengeti closed to tourists, have close encounters with lions and rhino, learn to pilot a plane in the bush, and generally soak up Africa.

The huge question that kept hitting me in the face was "How is Tanzania – how is all of Africa – going to develop economically while keeping its vast quantity and diversity of animals and ecosystems?" The huge herds of wildebeest were not going to make it in a few parks the size of Yellowstone or Yosemite in the United States. I decided I wanted to watch "development" happen around the world. I wanted to write about it, and how it could be balanced with protecting the environment. So I cancelled plans for law school and became a journalist.

It was good timing. I got a job in New York with Reuters, the British news agency, in 1972, hired because I had taught in a British education system in East Africa and was deemed to be fluent in both American and English, languages my English bosses perceived as quite different. The year 1972 also marked the UN environment conference in Stockholm. The gathering "raised awareness", but failed to convince a lot of developing-world governments, who saw concern over plants and animals as a luxury they could not afford. Brazil became a sort of spokes-government for this view, arguing that pollution meant money. They were happy to have more pollution and less rainforest if they could have the economic prosperity that seemed to go with pollution in the wealthier North.

Reuters took me to London and made me global science editor, despite my never having studied science. ("You won't write over anyone's head," said the editor.) I spent several happy years covering science around the world: climbing into Soviet fusion reactors, travelling the drylands of the western Sudan witnessing the sands flowing in over people's homes (a process caused by overuse of fragile drylands that the French would label *desertification*), and trying not to appear stupid talking to Nobel laureates about the universe's first two minutes after the Big Bang.

It was also a good time to watch and write about the environment/development debate. Scientists were beginning to worry seriously about the loss of species and of habitats such as the rainforests and coral reefs, about climate change, desertification, and overuse of topsoil and fresh water.

In 1980, these alarming trends were gathered together by the US government and reported in a book called *The Global 2000 Report to the President*. My old friend Gus Speth, who was with the Carter Administration then and is now dean of the Yale School of Forestry and Environmental Studies, published a book in 2004 in which he compared the trends reported and predicted in Global 2000 to present reality:

- population would grow from 4.5 billion then to 6.3 billion in 2000 (actual number in 2004, 6.3 billion);
- tropical forests would be cut down at the rate of an acre a second (this is what has happened);
- some 15% to 20% of all species would be extinct by 2000, mostly due to tropical deforestation (extinction rates remain controversial, but Speth quotes several experts to show that the Global 2000 figure might have been a little high but was roughly right);

- about six million hectares a year of drylands were being rendered nearly barren by desertification (this rate continues today);
- Global 2000 had this to say about climate change: "If the projected rates of increase in fossil fuel combustion... were to continue, the doubling of the CO_2 content of the atmosphere could be expected after the middle of the next century... The result could be significant alterations in precipitation patterns around the world and a 2 degree to 3 degree Celsius rise in temperatures in the middle latitudes of the earth."[1] (This prediction holds today.)

The point is that we knew roughly the issues and the scale of their effects a quarter of a century ago. We have failed to act on all fronts. With knowledge comes responsibility. So this failure has been a global moral failure as well as a failure of political will.

Sustainable development

In the early 80s I pulled my career chair even closer to the environment/development debate and joined the International Institute for Environment and Development (IIED), a London-based think tank. At the time, there was a deep schism between environmentalists and "developmentalists". Many of the former wanted to halt economic growth to save the environment, at their most extreme arguing that it was wrong to vaccinate children in the developing world because population increase was bad for the environment. The Green groups back then gave hardly a thought to the poor, or the effects of their day-to-day struggle for food and firewood on the environment.

The development groups, and most governments, put people first and saw the destruction of forests, productive drylands and waterways as a reasonable price to be paid for economic development.

Barbara Ward, the wise woman who founded IIED, saw that people cannot pull themselves out of poverty in an impoverished environment and that the environment cannot be walled off from the effects of human activity. She identified a need to balance the two concerns, to organize the apparent trade-offs between economic development and environmental protection.

However, in the early 80s those paying attention began to notice a chilling syndrome. There was very little economic development.

Africa was sliding backwards; it was the "lost decade" in Latin America, and Asia had not begun to take off. But at the same time, environmental destruction was continuing apace. There was no trade-off; there was failure on both fronts.

From the United Nations' point of view, this meant that neither the UN Environment Programme nor the UN Development Programme was doing its job. Under pressure from various member countries, mainly the Scandinavians and Japan, the UN established the grandly titled World Commission on Environment and Development (WCED) and asked Norway's off-again-on-again Prime Minister Gro Harlem Brundtland to chair it and help pick about two dozen commissioners. In the mid-80s it began meeting and holding hearings around the world.

I was called in to help the Commission write its report, sitting in its meetings to try to turn the commissioners' observations and conclusions into readable prose.

The theme of the report, "sustainable development", had been used in the literature before but without clear definition. The Brundtland Commission, as it came to be called

(with Mrs. Brundtland earning the delightful title of "Madame Chairman"), defined it as forms of development that "meet the needs of the present without compromising the ability of future generations to meet their needs".

The concept is both extremely complex and extremely simple. Its complexity has led to myriad attempts to define it better. But in its simpler manifestations, it means things like "don't eat the seeds you need to plant for next year's harvest" and "don't burn down your house in winter to keep warm". On a global level, it meant "do not try to get richer by destroying life-support systems".

"Finally!" I thought. "Environment and development have finally been united in one phrase. Make progress today in ways that meet human needs but do not rob future generations of environmental resources such as clean air, drinkable water, topsoil, trees, and fish." We were a bit short of examples of sustainable development, but could offer a host of examples of current, unsustainable forms of "progress".

Energy use offered an excellent example of unsustainability. In 1980, global energy consumption stood at around 10 Terawatts

(TW) per year. A Terawatt is a billion kilowatts, and a Terawatt per year is roughly equivalent to burning a billion tonnes of coal. But forget the TW and think of the figure 10. If per capita energy use remained the same as in 1980 – that is, a European using 80 times the energy of a sub-Saharan African – then a population of 8.2 billion people in 2025 would need about 14TW, the Commission's report reckoned. That 40% increase seemed to assure serious climate change.

But, if the developing world actually developed along the carbon pathway of the industrial world and started using energy at the same rates as Europeans and North Americans, then the same global population would require 55TW. I suspected that a quintupling of energy use, mostly carbon fuels, would give earth the runaway greenhouse effect that rules the planet Venus.

However, there was a chilling logic to these figures that the Commission did not go into. They seemed to me to suggest three choices:

1. We could conserve energy and urgently develop and switch to new and renewable energy sources – wind, solar, hydro, wave, safe nuclear.

2. Or we in the industrial countries could tell the developing world that we had done the maths and, for the sake of the planet, they could not be allowed to develop. Sub-Saharan Africa, for example, would have to continue to cook on firewood, dung and straw.

3. Or we could do nothing – "business as usual" – and follow the carbon road into climate cataclysm.

To my naïve surprise, we chose the last option, business as usual. Economic development for as far ahead as we can see will be based mainly on carbon: coal, oil and gas.

The Commission's report, which was dubbed The Brundtland Report, published in 1987, called for the convening of an "earth summit" in five years; and to the astonishment of the commissioners, who did not expect to be taken seriously, the Earth Summit was duly held in Rio in 1992. Many heads of state duly attended, and awareness was duly raised. But the Earth Summit changed little.

In 1987, commissioners went home to their native countries where they had been ministers and chief scientists and spread the notion of sustainable development. The US commissioner was William Ruckelshaus, twice head of the US Environmental Protection Agency. He was a Republican, and Ronald Reagan was then the president of a Republican government that did not care much for either environment or development issues. So Ruckelshaus kept fairly quiet.

Mrs. Brundtland, then once again prime minister of Norway, by chance had a state visit to the US scheduled right after her report was published. Her aides were warned by Reagan's aides that she should not mention the findings of her report. The US bureaucrats were not afraid that Reagan would disagree; they were afraid that in what was rapidly becoming his dotage, he would embrace the concept of sustainable development and thus upset US policies. So the concept never gained much foothold in the United States.

The rain today
In fact, sustainable development never caught on among policy-makers anywhere, except for use in speeches. We are far from meeting the needs of the present and far from giving any serious policy thought to the needs of future, larger generations.

This failure has led to the multi-pronged calamity, or clash of calamities, that I alluded to at the beginning – the hard rain that is falling now and is going to get worse.

First, most of the world is poor, and over one-sixth of the global population is suffering "extreme" or "absolute" poverty, the sort of poverty that kills.

Second, a few big countries have suddenly started to develop economically, but in the old-fashioned carbon-based, resource-raping methods of the European Industrial Revolution.

Third, our political systems are wholly inadequate, or inappropriate, to manage these challenges. So the three prongs of the present crisis (from the Greek word *krisis*, meaning "time to choose") are people, planet and political systems.

People

Sustainable development is a more radical concept than most people realize in that its first clause calls for meeting the needs of the present. That is not happening.

There are various definitions and numbers associated with world poverty. One of the simplest is a World Bank estimation that 11%

of the world's people are well-off; 11% have a moderate income, and 78% are poor.[2] But that includes various levels of poverty. Almost half the people on earth (nearly three billion) try to exist on the equivalent of less than $2 a day. The absolute poor try to exist on the equivalent of $1 a day. There are 1.1 billion of these people.

They cannot meet their basic needs – food, clean water, shelter – and by definition not meeting basic needs often leads to premature death. This is roughly the same billion who entered the new millennium unable to read or write, thus with little hope of escaping poverty. Their children tend to die in large numbers – about 1.7 million every year due to old diseases like diarrhoea and sleeping sickness. Their rain is now.

Poverty statistics are often mind-numbing and impossible to relate to individual lives. The Gross Domestic Product of the poorest 48 nations (about a quarter of the world's countries) is less than the wealth of the world's three richest *people* combined. In 1820 the richest country was three times richer than the poorest country; by the 1990s, the richest country was 72 times richer than the poorest.

The one-fifth of the world's population that lives in the "rich world" consumes 86% of the world's goods.

It is outrageous, grossly unfair, horribly short-sighted, and no way to run a planet. And few of us notice.

Poor people simply cannot live sustainably; they are forced to overuse and degrade scarce resources, whether firewood or topsoil or water in arid areas. Countries with majorities of poor citizens cannot afford honest, effective government, infrastructure such as roads and communications systems, education and healthcare. Thus they do not attract foreign investment. It is as hard for a poor country to pull itself out of poverty as for a poor person.

It is sometimes claimed that poverty spawns terrorism. In fact terrorists often simply use poverty as an excuse for their actions. But there are links. Poor countries tend to be more unstable. Poverty and instability are part of the syndrome of "failed states". Such states tend to breed or harbour violence and terrorism. In the failed states of Africa, this terror stays mostly in-country, sending refugees over borders into neighbouring states. The terrorism harboured in the failed state of Afghanistan became global in 2001.

Celebrity US economist Jeffrey Sachs was right in spirit then he wrote: "Since Sept. 11, 2001, the US has launched a war on terrorism, but it has neglected the deeper causes of global instability. The nearly $5 billion that the US will spend this year on the military will never buy lasting peace if the US continues to spend only one-thirtieth of that, around $16 million, to address the plight of the poorest of the poor, whose societies are destabilized by extreme poverty."[3]

The wealthier countries have actually developed policies that keep poor countries poor. They mostly come in the form of rich countries using their muscle and wealth to keep weaker, poorer countries from competing with them. The US and Europe pay their rich farmers $300 billion a year to overproduce commodities such as cotton and sugar, thereby lowering world prices for poor farmers in poor countries. When international treaties are negotiated, rich countries send delegations of dozens of lawyers and experts, overwhelming the one or two delegates poor countries can afford or find.

At the time of writing the Doha round of world trade talks is stalled, mainly over issues of agricultural subsidies, tariffs and barriers. Economists agree that a fairer, more liberal world trade system would pump billions more dollars into that system, most of it going to the wealthier countries. But these countries are too blinded by their own short-term, knee-jerk competitiveness even to act in their own self-interest. Today the 20% living in the world's wealthier countries enjoy 82% of the expanding export trade and 68% of foreign direct investment; the bottom fifth of the world's population benefits from about 1% of global trade.

There is much talk about increasing foreign aid to help countries meet the Millennium Assessment Goals, a set of targets hammered together by the UN in 2000, which include reducing by half the proportion of people living on less than a dollar a day, reducing by half the proportion of people who suffer from hunger, and ensuring that all boys and girls complete a full course of primary schooling. Most of these goals are meant to be reached by 2015, but almost as soon as they were announced, experts began to report on how little progress was being made.

There is much that poor countries can do to develop without spending great amounts of money: educate women and ensure that they have control of their own fertility, focus on domestic food security (rather than exports), and so on.

But development does require capital, and foreign aid has never been much help because it has never been proportional to the scale of the needs. Also, aid programmes are based first on the priorities of the giving nations, second on the priorities of companies in the giving nations, third on the priorities of the recipient nations' governments (i.e. the élite, whose priorities tend not to have much to do with the priorities of their poorest citizens). The poor, the rhetorical focus of all aid, are only a fourth-level priority. Aid simply cannot get through all the other filters to reach the poor.

Terrorism is important to this debate for another reason. Who could have imagined that the US would have responded to the September 11 attack by invading a country that had absolutely nothing to do with it and had no weapons of mass destruction to threaten the US or anyone else? It bombed civilians. It imprisoned and tortured citizens, using the techniques of ex-dictator Saddam Hussein. It allowed the looting of cultural treasures and the destruction of crucial infrastructure.

All of this has turned the Iraq War into a machine producing an almost limitless supply of terrorists who hate the United States and the West. In mid-2005 a leaked US Central Intelligence Agency report registered its concern that the Iraq conflict was pulling in disaffected young people from around the Muslim world and turning them into skilled insurgents. Their skills will eventually be used elsewhere. Chronic terrorism will continue to keep poverty and the environment at the bottom of the issue priority list.

Planet

In the early 1990s, I left IIED to work for Swiss billionaire Stephan Schmidheiny, who wanted to spend a lot of his money promoting sustainable development; I helped him set up a foundation to do so.

We put some of the first money into a bold and brash idea: a scientific survey of all of the planet's ecosystems. The plan was sparked by the fear that while global warming was a real threat, a more alarming and immediate threat was the decline of ecosystems and the effects of this on human society.

So the survey, eventually taken on officially by the UN in 2000 and involving over 1,360 scientists, did not simply look at the health of plants, animals and pristine parkland, but at the quality of the services that ecosystems provide to human beings.

It announced its findings in March 2005. About 60% (15 out of 24) of the ecosystem services studied are being degraded or used unsustainably, including freshwater "capture fisheries" (wild fish as opposed to farmed fish), air and water purification, the regulation of regional and local climate, natural hazards and pests.

This degradation of our life-support systems could accelerate rapidly during the first half of this century and "is a barrier to achieving the Millennium Development Goals", the survey report said. It could also lead to "accelerating, abrupt, potentially irreversible changes", examples of which include "disease emergence, abrupt alterations in water quality, the creation of 'dead zones' in coastal waters, the collapse of fisheries, and shifts in regional climate". The losses of ecosystem services "are being borne disproportionately by the poor, are contributing to growing inequities and disparities across groups of people, and are sometimes the principal factor causing poverty and social conflict".

The crises are thus connected: environmental breakdown causes poverty and social conflict, and poverty and social conflict cause environmental breakdown.

Did such alarming news, released simultaneously around the world, alarm citizens and decision-makers? No, it alarmed only the scientists involved in the study. The *New York Times*, usually sound on these issues, published nothing on the day of release, saving it for an inside piece in its science section almost a week later. The front page of that science section was devoted to interesting facts about snake venom. If such news is not deemed important by news reporters, then how can society be expected to organize to cope with the threats?

Climate change remains the summation of all environmental threats. Our modern world is delicate and finely balanced; almost any change is a shock. Changes in rainfall and sunlight will upset finely calibrated farming systems. Forests and grasslands and reefs will perish as they are unable to adapt fast enough.

Old diseases in new places will upset health systems. I moved back to the United States in the early part of this millennium and watched the alarm that a few cases of West Nile Virus caused in New York City. As climate changes, "tropical" diseases such as malaria, dengue fever, snail fever and others will all start spreading.

We think of climate change as gradual, a slow rise in temperature and in sea levels. Yet nature can be awfully sudden: water remains liquid right up the temperature scale until suddenly at 100 degrees Celsius it becomes steam. Pouring a lot of extra energy into the atmosphere could have relatively sudden consequences; predictions include a reversal of the Atlantic Gulf Stream, which would leave temperate parts of North America and north Europe with a climate more like Siberia's; a melting of the Arctic permafrost could release enough trapped methane to radically accelerate the warming. Our grandchildren may be the first to learn whether these worries were justifiable.

There have been numerous studies of ways of coping with and decreasing the effects of climate change. Most involve a mix of approaches – more use of gas, nuclear, new and renewable energy sources; more energy-efficient vehicles and buildings; capturing and storing carbon emissions. None of these reports has been paid any serious attention. We continue to choose "business as usual".

Energy demand could double by the year 2050, and rapidly developing countries such as China and India are building coal-fired power plants to provide that energy. Carbon hangs around in the atmosphere for about a century, so much of what is there now will be joined by new gases over the coming decades. We have already laid the momentum for those "abrupt, potentially irreversible changes".

Politics

When George W. Bush ran for president in 2000, he promised federal limits on greenhouse gas emissions. Once elected, he changed his mind, labelling the science "incomplete". In 2002, the US EPA sent a 260-page report to the UN summing up US research into climate change. The report predicted that growing greenhouse gas emissions could warm the United States by several degrees Celsius during the 21st century. Bush dismissed the report as something issued by "the bureaucracy".

Thus we have in the United States a fundamentalist president who governs by hunch, who does not listen to anyone not in agreement with him, and who is capable of casually contradicting his best scientists. Much more frightening than that, the great majority of the general public is not alarmed at any of this.

Other heads of government talk more coherently about environmental issues, especially climate change. Jacques Chirac says it is "absolutely obvious that global warming has started". Tony Blair has made it one of his prime talking points. Indeed, the newspapers and other media of Europe are full of sensible accounts of environment and development challenges and appropriate responses.

But little is done. For some time it has seemed as if the other leaders were comfortable blaming US intransigence for their own inability to act.

It is emotionally satisfying to note the crucial issues with which politicians are not dealing and accuse them of stupidity, short-sightedness, political cowardice. But in an odd way, they are realists, reacting appropriately to the realities of the political systems we have created. I used to troop up to Capitol Hill in Washington every now and then to testify before some Congressional committee on issues such as African poverty, population, or desertification. I would suggest things to be done. Afterwards, members of Congress would say privately, "Of course, you are right. But there are just no votes in it. No one gets elected in this country promising to fix African poverty."

That is the bottom line. Our democracies have a hard time doing anything novel for which there are few votes, such as mitigating climate change, better managing ecosystems, or creating a global trading system that would help poor countries develop. There are not nearly enough votes in the US, or Europe, or anywhere else. We have the knowledge, data and technologies to do all of those things. And doing them would probably save money and decrease terror and destruction over time. But there are no votes.

US Vice-President Al Gore nailed his colours to the environmental mast when in office by publishing a book called *Earth in the Balance: Ecology and the Human Spirit*. But when he ran for president in 2000 he kept his mouth pretty firmly shut about such issues. There are no votes.

There are brief eruptions that look almost like change. The July 2005 Gleneagles summit of the G8 nations (the wealthy) looked set to make progress on climate change. The European leaders almost promised progress. The chairman's summary of the meeting said, "All of us agreed that climate change is happening now, that human activity is contributing to it, and that it could affect every part of the globe." It added that "we resolved to take urgent action to meet the challenges we face."

What is that action? It is "a new Dialogue between the G8 nations and other countries with significant energy needs, consistent with the aims and principles of the UN Framework Convention on Climate Change."

Michael McCarthy, environment editor for the *Independent* newspaper in the UK wrote after the meeting that the agreement to talk to the leading developing nations, whose greenhouse emissions are rapidly increasing, "is the most important step to counter climate change since the signing of the Kyoto Protocol in 1997".[4] The tragedy is that he is right. So very little is happening that those concerned about these issues now numbly grasp at straws and report "progress".

Business as usual

How can we be so stupid, so short-sighted? How can we ignore the suffering of billions, the threats to other species, and the links between the two?

The answer is bleakly simple: we cannot get these issues on our political radar screens. The poor, the majority in many developing countries, have little or no political power. Those with political power are not affected. Democracy cannot seem to cope with serious, complex issues that do not affect voters' daily lives, and yet democracy is the best political system available.

I will not be killed by climate change or poverty. I am passionate about these issues because as a young man I chose to watch them, and have been held spellbound for the past 40 years at our failure to cope with them.

The question that got me started – how can Tanzania develop without destroying its environmental assets? – has not been answered over all those years. There were about 15 million Tanzanians when I lived there. There are about 37 million today. That population growth has taken its toll on natural habitat. Although the national income per head is only $290 – well below a dollar a day, and low even for Africa – the economy has been growing rapidly lately, and some commentators see it poised for an economic take-off. Yet there is no concern in Tanzania about the sustainability of such a take-off.

When Ethiopia and a swath of countries south of the Sahara sank into drought and famine in the mid-1980s, Irish rocker Bob Geldof organized the Band Aid single and Live Aid concerts and raised millions of dollars for Africa. He asked me to form a committee to help spend the money. We thought back then that famine would never be allowed in Africa again after all this attention. But it has come and gone regularly there over the past 20 years. As the leaders deliberated in Scotland, and as a gracefully ageing Geldof demanded action, children were dying steadily of hunger in Niger.

The question now is not so much "How could we have learned so little in all these years?" but "How could we have learned so much and done so little?" We understand the causes and cures of environmental degradation. We know roughly how nations pull themselves out of poverty.

Dylan's song was prophetic almost half a century ago. Now the prophecy has been, and is being, chillingly fulfilled: "sad forests", "dead oceans", "where the people are many and their hands are all empty", "where hunger is ugly, where souls are forgotten".

How did he get it so right so long ago? It is not too late to listen and act. But we will neither listen nor act.

Lloyd Timberlake
Washington, DC, 2006

1 James Gustave Speth, *Red Sky at Morning: America and the Crisis of the Global Environment* (New Haven, CT, 2004, Yale University Press)

2 Branko Milanovic and Shlomo Yitzhaki, "Decomposing World Income Distribution: Does the World Have a Middle Class?" (Washington, DC, 2001, The World Bank)

3 Jeffrey Sachs, "The End of Poverty", *Time*, New York: March 14, 2005, Vol. 165, Iss. 11, pg. 42

4 Michael McCarthy, "Most important move on the environment since Kyoto", *Independent*, London: July 9, 2005

What'll you do now?
Afterword

The main purpose of *Hard Rain* is to prove wrong Lloyd Timberlake's assertion in these pages that our democratic political systems cannot solve the related tragedies of environmental destruction and human poverty.

Lloyd's essay is helpful for two reasons. It shows just how tough the problems are. And it begins to crack the "conspiracy of hope" – the demand by editors that books, articles, and programmes on any intractable issue end on an upbeat message of optimism. Hope is good; the late environment and development guru Barbara Ward even argued that "we have a duty to hope"; but this media convention of happy endings lulls people into the false belief that "the grown-ups know about it; it's all going to be all right".

But it is not going to be all right, for all the reasons Lloyd points out, without a huge, prolonged popular uprising.

It is fun to blame the politicians, but we elected them. And if we did not vote personally for the short-sighted leaders now in power, then our relatives, neighbours, friends and co-workers did. Let us begin by gently converting those nearby.

What *we* are going to do now in the way of gentle conversion is send copies of this book to national leaders and global opinion-makers, with the letter overleaf. It is a start.

Where will you start? You could do the obvious things. Turn off the light. Buy long-life bulbs. Turn down the heat; put on a sexy sweater. Walk. Ride a bike. Buy a hybrid car, if you need a car. Turn off the water while you are brushing your teeth.

These things are part of walking lightly on the planet, and part of setting examples. Note that some of these things are actually fun. It has been argued that California contains such a high percentage of eco-nuts because it also contains a high percentage of hedonists. And saving the planet – walking, demonstrating, saving water by showering together – can be fun.

Then there are the less obvious things. Join a big environment or development group. Write a letter a day: to a newspaper, a politician, a CEO. Support a movement. Attack a stupid movement.

Specialize. Do you like birds, plants, a nearby stream? Read up. Conserve what you like. Now that you have joined a big national or international organization, join a local group of birders or friends of the local creek.

Like outdoor sports? Hiking, fishing, hunting… even gardening? Work to conserve the wilderness, waters, creatures, topsoil and predictable climate that make all these activities possible.

Like to travel? Go to Kenya and see the elephants and rhino and then visit the slums of Nairobi and see what is happening. Talk to the groups working locally. You'll find an odd mix of despair and hope. Trek the Andes in Bolivia and then visit the vast El Alto neighborhoods above La Paz. Be aware of the best and worst of modern living – and arrange to absorb the carbon you burn as you go.

You may choose to begin your journey by exploring the websites, books and journals we list in "The Bigger Picture" on pages 108 to 117. You could also come and visit us at hardrainproject.com.

Whatever you do, make it your own, true to your own self, enriching, satisfying. Do not set an example of joyless martyrdom.

Are your religious? There is not a single religion that is not wrapped around a core of compassion for the poor, the hungry and the

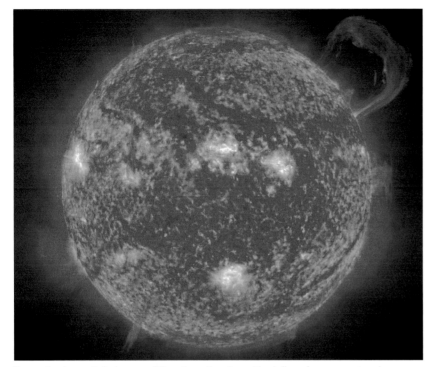

The sun. A vast amount of solar energy falls on the earth each year. The challenge for governments and industry is to harness more of the sun's energy using solar panels, wind turbines and hydroelectric generators. Fusion reactors that mimic the way the sun generates heat may supply future generations with energy that is environmentally safe and economically attractive. © NASA/Jet Propulsion Laboratory.

downtrodden. How can the US leaders profess Christian beliefs while giving tax breaks to the rich and being so comparatively miserly with aid? How can the Christian cultures of Europe be so heedless of the poor in their suburbs and former colonies? Why do Muslim, Hindu, Buddhist, Jewish and atheist leaders do no better? Let us put a little compassion and love back in our religions and politics. And let us show a little more care for the planet that our various gods created, if we believe in various gods.

Do it where you are – obviously in your home and garden and neighbourhood, but also in your workplace. The problem is not so much that our politicians are in the pockets of corporations, but that they are in the pockets of the worst corporations, the ones that need subsidies and tax breaks and government contracts.

Many of the most successful corporations are trying to figure out what their "corporate social responsibility" is, to do it, and to report on it. Some are even trying to figure out how to do business with the poor in ways that benefit the poor. Nudge your company in the right direction. If you cannot, leave. Why spend your time on earth working for the bad guys?

Howard Gardner, psychologist, professor of education at Harvard and a professor of neurology at Boston University Medical School, has written books describing leadership as telling stories that others believe and follow.

Get out and tell that story of the hard, hurting rain; what is causing it; how to stop it.

Still Pictures Moving Words, 2006

To whom it may concern

An open letter to world leaders

On the page opposite, we present the full text of a letter that was sent to world leaders, along with a copy of this book, immediately before publication. We also sent copies to leading journalists, environmental commentators, business leaders, government ministers and their advisors. We will post all replies on the hardrainproject.com website.

We welcome contributions from all readers, so come along to hardrainproject.com, have a browse and post your comments. We look forward to meeting you there.

Dear World Leader

We offer in these pages disturbing pictures to accompany disturbing words written more than 40 years ago.

Bob Dylan saw a hard, hurting rain coming, destructive to people, plants, animals, forests, oceans, and streams. Oddly, scientists agreed with the young singer. They began warning at about the time Dylan was writing his song of linked human and environmental degradation.

Today's science agrees with yesterday's science. In 2005, more than 1,000 researchers assessing the planet's ecosystems warned that most of them are losing their ability to serve human needs. More than one billion people live in absolute poverty, a poverty that kills many of them, including the 1.7 million children who die each year from preventable diseases. Environmental and human poverty reinforce and feed off one another.

Yet you – and we – do little or nothing.

As democracy has spread to almost all countries over the past 40 years, responsibility for national action falls to the people that leaders serve. However, we are learning that democracy does not work for the important, complex, long-term issues such as ecosystem loss, mass poverty, and global trade because regular elections ensure we pay attention only to the short-term, the visible and the nearby.

These are the sorts of issues that require leadership, require visionaries who can see the real threats behind complex syndromes and can explain these to people, build coalitions, and lay out solutions. Such leadership is non-existent today.

Our book is an appeal to you, and an appeal to readers to get in touch with you and ask for your attention, for you to demonstrate the responsibility you promise when you ask for our votes or support.

Please lead your people toward forms of progress that sustain all of humanity, while sustaining the planet.

We would welcome your response to this letter, to this book, and to the collision with nature described in its pages. If you don't have time to write a formal letter, please email us at the address below.

Yours sincerely,

Mark Edwards
Lloyd Timberlake
replies@hardrainproject.com

The bigger picture

Further reading

Organizations and websites

African Development Bank Group
The ADB Group is a multinational development finance institution established in 1964 to foster economic growth and social progress in Africa.
www.afdb.org

Alliance to Save Energy
Founded in 1977, the ASE is a non-profit coalition of business, government, environmental and consumer leaders promoting energy-efficiency policies that minimize costs to society and individual consumers, whilst lessening greenhouse gas emissions and their impact on the global climate.
www.ase.org

Amnesty International
Amnesty International is an independent worldwide movement of people who campaign for internationally recognized human rights, whether connected to corrupt governance, false imprisonment, workers' rights or violence in the home.
www.amnesty.org

Asian Development Bank
ADB is a multilateral development finance institution which aims to reduce poverty in Asia and the Pacific. Established in 1966, it is owned by 63 members mostly from the region.
www.adb.org

BobDylan.com
The official Dylan website offers news, tour updates, full discography and song lyrics, book reviews and links to related information.
www.bobdylan.com

Botanic Gardens Conservation International
Founded in 1987 to link botanic gardens as a co-operating global network for effective plant conservation, BGCI now includes over 500 member institutions in 112 countries, working together to implement a worldwide strategy for plant conservation.
www.bgci.org.uk

Center for Media and Democracy
A non-profit organization that seeks to strengthen democracy by promoting media that are "of, by and for the people". Their projects include the quarterly investigative journal, *PR Watch*, books by staff members, Spin of the Day, an online daily report on spin and propaganda in the news; and SourceWatch, a wiki-based investigative journalism resource to which anyone can contribute.
www.prwatch.org

CICERO
The Center for International Climate and Environmental Research - Oslo, founded by the Norwegian government in 1990, is an independent research centre associated with the University of Oslo. CICERO's mandate is to conduct research and provide information about issues of climate change.
www.cicero.uio.no

Climate Care
Climate Care offers organizations and individuals a way to reduce their impact on global warming by selling them carbon offsets, which balance out CO_2 emissions by reducing an equivalent amount elsewhere. These reductions are made through projects that provide renewable energy, energy efficiency or reforestation, and improve the lives of the world's poorest. The website's CO_2 Calculators allow easy assessment of emissions from flying, driving and domestic energy.
www.climatecare.org

ClimateWire.org
An international news service focusing on climate change, delivered by RTCC and UNEP/GRID-Arendal.
www.climatewire.org

CO_2 Science
A weekly review and repository of scientific research findings related to carbon dioxide and global change.
www.co2science.org

Comparative Research Programme on Poverty
CROP is an international NGO started in 1992 by the International Social Science Council, part of UNESCO. Its aim is to produce sound and reliable knowledge, which can serve as a basis for poverty reduction.
www.crop.org

Contrails
A website dedicated to studying the effects of condensation trails, also known as aviation smog.
www.contrails.nl

Convention on Biological Diversity
Signed by 150 government leaders at the 1992 Rio Earth Summit, this convention aims to promote sustainable development. It recognizes that biological diversity is about more than plants, animals and micro-organisms and their ecosystems. It is about people and their need for food security, medicines, fresh air, water, shelter and a clean and healthy environment in which to live.
www.biodiv.org

Debt AIDS Trade Africa
DATA aims to raise awareness about and spark responses to the crises swamping Africa: unpayable debts, the uncontrolled spread of AIDS, and unfair trade rules that keep Africans poor.
www.data.org

Development Gateway
The Development Gateway Foundation aims to improve people's lives in developing countries by building partnerships and information systems that provide access to knowledge for development.
www.developmentgateway.org

Earth Institute
The Earth Institute at Columbia University is the world's leading academic centre for the study, teaching and implementation of sustainable development, placing special emphasis on the needs of the world's poor.
www.earthinstitute.columbia.edu

Earth Policy Institute
Founded by Lester Brown, formerly founder and president of the Worldwatch Institute, the goal of the EPI is to raise public awareness and support an effective public response to the threats posed by continuing population growth, rising CO_2 emissions, the loss of plant and animal species, and the many other trends that are adversely affecting the earth.
www.earth-policy.org

Earthscan
Earthscan/James & James publishes a wide range of books, magazines and journals on all aspects of sustainable development, including *Climate Policy*, a peer-reviewed journal focusing on responses to climate change.
www.earthscan.co.uk

Earthwatch Institute
Earthwatch Institute engages the public worldwide in scientific field research and education, to promote the understanding and action necessary for a sustainable environment.
www.earthwatch.org

Energy Saving Trust
A non-profit organization set up after the 1992 Rio Earth Summit, EST works with households, business and the public sector to encourage a more efficient use of energy, stimulate the demand and supply of cleaner fuelled vehicles, and to promote the use of small-scale renewable energy sources, such as solar and wind power.
www.est.org.uk

Environmentalists for Nuclear Energy
Arguments in favour of the nuclear option, including a link to James Lovelock's international homepage.
www.ecelo.org and **www.ecelo.org/lovelock**

Eden Project
Based in the UK, the Eden Project is an educational charitable trust that aims to promote the understanding and responsible management of the vital relationship between plants, people and resources, leading to a sustainable future for all.
www.edenproject.com

Eldis
The Eldis Gateway to Development Information is an internet-based information service, filtering, structuring and presenting development information via the web and email. It has a large library of online documents and a directory of development-related internet services.
www.eldis.org

Envirolink
The EnviroLink Network is a non-profit organization that has been providing access to thousands of online environmental resources since 1991.
www.envirolink.org

Environmental Media Services
EMS is a non-profit communications clearing house dedicated to expanding media coverage of critical environmental and public health issues. It was founded in 1994 by former *Time*, *Newsweek* and *Sports Illustrated* journalist Arlie Schardt.
www.ems.org

EnviroTruth.org
This website was set up in 2002 by the National Center for Public Policy Research to counter environmentalist groups that "have seized the world stage and the public's attention by distorting facts, bending the truth and even committing acts of terrorism against innocent citizens". This is one of the few websites where you can read and assess arguments that go against the environmental consensus.
www.envirotruth.org

European Commission Environment Directorate
Europe's Environment Directorate is hostage to its mission statement: "Protecting, preserving and improving the environment for present and future generations, and promoting sustainable development."
europa.eu.int/comm/environment

Forum for the Future
Forum for the Future is recognized as the UK's leading sustainable development charity. It was founded in 1996 by environmentalists Jonathon Porritt, Sara Parkin and Paul Ekins with the object of accelerating the building of a sustainable way of life, and to overcome the many barriers to more sustainable practice.
www.forumforthefuture.org.uk

Friends of the Earth
Friends of the Earth has been campaigning on
environmental issues since 1969. Its international
federation is the world's largest grassroots
environmental network, uniting 71 diverse national
member groups and some 5,000 local activist groups
on every continent.
www.foe.co.uk and www.foei.org

G8
The Group of Eight leading industrialized nations
(Canada, France, Germany, Italy, Japan, Russia, UK and
US) meets informally on an annual basis for discussions
aimed at boosting co-operation over trade and finance,
strengthening the global economy, promoting peace
and democracy and preventing or resolving conflicts.
Presidency rotates between the partner nations, and
Britain's presidency in 2005 brought climate change
and world poverty high on the agenda. The University
of Toronto hosts a comprehensive information centre
with links to host websites.
www.g8.utoronto.ca

Global Call to Action against Poverty
GCAP is a worldwide alliance of community groups,
trade unions, individuals, religious and faith groups
and campaigners who want to make world leaders live
up to their promises and to make a lasting difference in
the fight against poverty.
www.whiteband.org

Global Environment Facility
Established in 1991, GEF aims to help developing
countries fund projects and programmes that protect
the global environment. GEF grants support projects
related to biodiversity, climate change, international
waters, land degradation, the ozone layer and
persistent organic pollutants.
www.gefweb.org

Global Warming International Center
A California-based international body disseminating
information on global warming science and policy,
serving governmental agencies, NGOs and industry.
www.globalwarming.net

Green Car Congress
Green Car Congress offer news and analysis of the
energy choices, technologies, products, issues and
policies related to sustainable mobility.
www.greencarcongress.com

Green House Network
GHN wants to stop global warming, especially by
lobbying to change US government policy at state
and federal level.
www.greenhousenet.org

Greenpeace
Established in 1971, Greenpeace exists to expose
environmental criminals and to challenge governments
and corporations when they fail to live up to their
mandate to safeguard the world's environment and
its future.
www.greenpeace.org

Hard Rain Project
Find dates and venues for *Hard Rain* exhibitions, keep
up-to-date with the issues covered in the book, and
post your comments here. Copies of this book were
sent to heads of state and other men and women of
influence ahead of publication. The website will publish
their responses.
www.hardrainproject.com

Intergovernmental Panel on Climate Change
The IPCC was established by the WMO and UNEP
to assess scientific, technical and socio-economic
information relevant for the understanding of
climate change, its potential impacts and options
for adaptation and mitigation.
www.ipcc.ch

International Emissions Trading Association
The IETA is a non-profit organization created in 1999
to establish a functional international framework for
trading greenhouse gas emission reductions.
www.ieta.org

International Energy Agency
The IEA is an intergovernmental body which aims
to advance the security of energy supply, economic
growth and environmental sustainability through
energy policy co-operation.
www.iea.org

International Fund for Agricultural Development
IFAD, based in Italy, was founded in 1977 to work with
rural populations in developing countries to eliminate
poverty, hunger and malnutrition; raise productivity
and incomes, and improve the quality of rural lives.
www.ifad.org

International Institute for Environment and Development
Founded by Barbara Ward in 1971, IIED is an multi-
disciplinary policy research institute working towards
more sustainable and equitable global development.
www.iied.org

International Institute for Sustainable Development
Founded in 1990, IISD offers policy recommendations
to organizations such as the United Nations on
subjects including international trade and investment,
economic policy, climate change, measurement,
assessment and natural resources management.
www.iisd.org

International Monetary Fund
The IMF is an organization of 184 countries working to
foster global monetary co-operation, secure financial
stability, facilitate international trade, reduce poverty
and promote high employment and sustainable
economic growth.
www.imf.org

Internews
Internews is an international NGO working to improve
access to information for people around the world
by fostering independent media, promoting open
communications policies, and training journalists in
poor or disaster-hit communities.
www.internews.org

Kyoto Protocol
(see *United Nations Framework Convention on Climate
Change*)

MacArthur Foundation
The John D. and Catherine T. MacArthur Foundation
is a private, independent grant-making institution
that aims to help groups and individuals foster lasting
improvement in the human condition.
www.macfound.org

Make Poverty History
Aimed at governments, MPH gives a voice to the many
millions of people around the world who are demanding
action to end poverty.
www.makepovertyhistory.org

Médécins Sans Frontières
MSF is an international medical aid agency committed
to delivering emergency medical supplies wherever
they are needed, and raising awareness of the plight of
people whose health and livelihoods are threatened by
disease, famine, poverty, war or displacement.
www.msf.org

NASA
An exhaustive resource on the US space agency's
past, present and future explorations, and of the
earth's place in the universe. An extensive picture
and multimedia archive includes constantly updated
satellite imagery.
www.nasa.gov

Natural Resources Defense Council
A US environmental action organization that uses
law, science and the support of more than a million
members and activists to protect the planet's wildlife
and wild places.
www.nrdc.org

Natural Step
An international non-profit educational organization,
The Natural Step works to accelerate global
sustainability by guiding companies, communities
and governments onto an ecologically, socially and
economically sustainable path.
www.naturalstep.org

New Partnership for Africa's Development
NEPAD offers a vision and strategic framework for
Africa's renewal. It aims to eradicate poverty; to place
African countries, both individually and collectively,
on a path of sustainable growth and development; to
halt the marginalization of Africa in the globalization
process and enhance its integration into the global
economy, and to accelerate the empowerment of
women.
www.nepad.org

One
The One campaign is an effort to rally Americans
to fight the emergency of global AIDS and extreme
poverty by committing an additional one per cent of
the US budget to provide basic needs in the world's
poorest countries, and fight the corruption that wastes
valuable resources.
www.one.org

Organic Consumers Association
The OCA is an online and grassroots non-profit public
interest organization campaigning for health, justice
and sustainability. It is the leading voice in the US
promoting the views and interests of the nation's
estimated 50 million organic and socially responsible
consumers.
www.organicconsumers.org

*Organisation for Economic Co-operation and
Development*
The OECD has 30 member countries committed to
democratic government and the market economy. Best
known for its publications and statistics, its work covers
economic and social issues from macroeconomics
to trade, education, development, and science and
innovation.
www.oecd.org

Oxfam
The former Oxford Committee for Famine Relief, established in Britain in 1942, has grown into an international group of independent NGOs dedicated to fighting poverty and related injustice around the world.
www.oxfam.org

Pew Center on Global Climate Change
The Pew Center was established in 1998 as a non-profit, non-partisan and independent organization that provides information and innovative solutions in an effort to address global climate change.
www.pewclimate.org

Planet Ark
Planet Ark is an Australian not-for-profit organization working in partnership with businesses and organizations to bring about environmental change. It is best known internationally for its daily World Environment News service, sponsored by Reuters.
www.planetark.com

Plantlife International
Plantlife is the only charity dedicated exclusively to conserving wild plants and fungi in their natural habitats across the world.
www.plantlife.org.uk

Poverty Action Lab
Started in June 2003 by three professors at the Massachusetts Institute of Technology, PAL's objective is to improve the effectiveness of poverty programmes by providing policy-makers with scientific results that help shape successful policies to combat poverty. It works with NGOs, international organizations and others to evaluate programmes and disseminate the results of their research.
www.povertyactionlab.org

Rainforest Action Network
Founded in 1985, the Rainforest Action Network campaigns for tropical rainforests, their inhabitants and the natural systems that sustain life through grassroots organizing, education and non-violent direct action.
www.ran.org

Red Cross and Red Crescent
Established in 1863, the International Committee of the Red Cross is the force behind the International Red Cross and Red Crescent movements, whose humanitarian mission is to protect the lives and dignity of victims of war and internal violence and to provide them with assistance through a programme of responsive relief activities.
www.icrc.org and www.ifrc.org

Resources for the Future
A Washington-based independent institute dedicated to analyzing environmental, energy, and natural resource topics, RFF has influenced environmental policymaking worldwide since 1952. Its internet resource Weathervane provides direct, online access to the most up-to-date findings.
www.rff.org and www.weathervane.rff.org

Responding to Climate Change
RTCC is a non-profit NGO and an official observer to the UN Climate Change negotiations. It develops information products and channels through which business, government and NGOs can learn more about the threat of climate change and global warming to the world's environment and formulate the most appropriate response.
www.rtcc.org and www.climate-change.tv

Royal Society
Founded in 1660 by Sir Christopher Wren and a dozen forward-thinking contemporaries, the Royal Society is an independent charitable academy dedicated to promoting scientific excellence and influencing international policy in the fields of engineering and technology.
www.royalsoc.ac.uk

SafeClimate for Business
SafeClimate is a joint project of the World Resources Institute and the Center for Environmental Leadership in Business, dedicated to helping business of all sizes understand and take action on climate change.
www.safeclimate.net

Schumacher College
An international centre for ecological studies based in the UK, the College holds courses for participants aged 20 to 80 from all over the world.
www.schumachercollege.org.uk

Scripps Institution of Oceanography
Founded in 1903, research at Scripps encompasses physical, chemical, biological, geological and geophysical studies of the oceans using its own research ships.
www.sio.ucsd.edu

Sierra Club
Founded in 1892, the Sierra Club is America's oldest, largest and most influential grassroots environmental organization. Publications include the bi-monthly *Sierra* magazine and *The Planet* activists' newsletter.
www.sierraclub.org

Soil Association

The Soil Association is the membership charity at the heart of the UK organic movement. Since 1946 it has worked to raise awareness about the positive health and environmental benefits of organic food and farming and to support farmers in organic food production.
www.soilassociation.org and www.whyorganic.org

Stephan Schmidheiny

Swiss philanthropist who founded the World Business Council for Sustainable Development and sustainable development foundation AVINA among others.
www.stephanschmidheiny.net

Still Pictures

Still Pictures, founded by Mark Edwards in 1985 based on his personal archive, has since expanded into the world's leading photo agency specializing in the environment, nature and Third World issues.
www.stillpictures.com

Still Pictures Moving Words

Look out for news of future titles on our website.
www.stillpicturesmovingwords.com

Survival International

Survival is the only international organization supporting tribal peoples worldwide. It was founded in 1969 in response to the massacres, land thefts and genocide taking place in the Brazilian Amazon in the name of economic growth. Survival works for tribal peoples' rights through education, advocacy and campaigning, and also offers tribal people themselves a platform from which to address the world.
www.survival-international.org

Tyndall Centre for Climate Change Research

The Tyndall Centre brings together scientists, economists, engineers and social scientists to develop sustainable responses to climate change through transdisciplinary research and dialogue.
www.tyndall.ac.uk

Union of Concerned Scientists

UCS is an independent non-profit alliance of more than 100,000 concerned citizens and scientists. It aims to augment scientific analysis with innovative thinking and committed citizen advocacy to build a cleaner, healthier environment and a safer world.
www.ucsusa.org

United Nations Convention to Combat Desertification

The UNCCD was adopted in Paris in 1994 and came into force in 1996. More than 179 countries are parties.
www.unccd.int

United Nations Development Programme

UNDP is the UN's global development network. It advocates change and connects countries to knowledge, experience and resources in order to help people build a better life. It is on the ground in 166 countries.
www.undp.org

United Nations Educational, Scientific and Cultural Organization

UNESCO was founded in 1945. Today it styles itself as "a laboratory of ideas and a standard-setter to forge universal agreements on emerging ethical issues".
www.unesco.org

United Nations Environment Programme

UNEP aims to provide leadership and encourage partnership in caring for the environment by inspiring, informing and enabling nations and peoples to improve their quality of life without compromising that of future generations.
www.unep.org

United Nations Framework Convention on Climate Change

The UNFCCC was established to consider what can be done to reduce global warming and to cope with any inevitable temperature increases. The Kyoto Protocol is a legally binding addition to the treaty containing more powerful measures to ensure compliance among member nations.
www.unfccc.int

US Climate Change Science Program

A coalition of US federal agencies, CCSP admits only of climate change that "scientific evidence indicates that these changes are likely the result of a complex interplay of several natural and human-related forces".
www.climatescience.gov

US Climate Change Technology Program

A multi-agency research and development programme for the development of climate change technology, linked to official US policy.
www.climatetechnology.gov

US Environmental Protection Agency

The federal agency that is charged to "protect human health and the natural environment" was established by the White House and Congress in 1970 in response to growing public demand for cleaner water, air and land.
www.epa.gov

US Geological Survey
America's largest biological science and civilian mapping agency, the USGS collects, monitors, analyzes, and provides scientific understanding about natural resource conditions, issues, and problems, and provides impartial scientific information to resource managers, planners, and other customers.
www.usgs.gov

US global climate change policy
Includes the full text of President Bush's cautious commitment to action "advancing a pro-growth, pro-development approach to addressing this important global challenge".
www.state.gov/g/oes/climate

US National Oceanic & Atmospheric Administration
NOAA runs NESDIS, which provides access to global environmental data from satellites and other sources to promote, protect and enhance the US economy, security, environment and quality of life.
www.nesdis.noaa.gov and www.noaa.gov

Weathervane
(see *Resources for the Future*)

World Bank
The World Bank Group is a development bank that provides loans, policy advice, technical assistance and knowledge-sharing services to low- and middle-income countries to reduce poverty. In June 2005 Paul Wolfowitz, best known as a key architect of the Iraq War, was installed as president.
www.worldbank.org

World Conservation Union (IUCN)
A conservation network, the World Conservation Union (also known as the International Union for the Conservation of Nature and Natural Resources) brings together 82 States, 111 government agencies, more than 800 NGOs, and some 10,000 scientists and experts from 181 countries.
www.iucn.org

World Development Movement
Founded in 1970, WDM is a democratic movement of individual supporters, campaigners and local groups working in partnership with other international organizations to campaign against the root causes of poverty, and develop positive policy options that support sustainable development.
www.wdm.org.uk

World Health Organization
The WHO is the UN's specialist agency for international health and welfare. Established in 1948 and governed by 192 Member States through the World Health Assembly, the WHO publishes books, papers and online reports on health matters from avian flu to air pollution.
www.who.int

World Meteorological Organization
The WMO is an intergovernmental organization with a membership of 187 member states and territories. It originated from the International Meteorological Organization (IMO), which was founded in 1873. Established by the UN in 1950, it is now the UN system's voice on the state and behaviour of the earth's atmosphere, its interaction with the oceans, the climate it produces and the resulting distribution of water resources.
www.wmo.ch

World Resources Institute
The WRI's mission is to move human society to live in ways that protect the earth's environment and its capacity to provide for the needs and aspirations of current and future generations.
www.wri.org and www.climatehotmap.org

World Trade Organization
The WTO is an international body established to promote free trade and settle trade disputes between member nations. At its heart is the belief that expanding globalization will raise living standards around the world.
www.wto.org

Worldwatch Institute
A leading source of information on the interactions between key environmental, social, and economic trends. Publications include the annual *State of the World* and *Vital Signs* books and the bi-monthly *World Watch* magazine.
www.worldwatch.org

WWF
In just over four decades, WWF (formerly the World Wildlife Fund) has become one of the world's largest and most respected independent conservation organizations. Its ultimate goal is to stop and eventually reverse environmental degradation and to build a future where people live in harmony with nature.
www.panda.org

Books (alphabetical, by author)

The Great Illusion by Sir Norman Angell, published by William Heinemann, 1909. The first book to show that military and political power give a nation no commercial advantage, that it is an economic impossibility for one nation to seize or destroy the wealth of another, or for one nation to enrich itself by subjugating another, written by a man who later became a Nobel Peace laureate and helped to found the League of Nations.

Understanding the Present by Brian Appleyard, published by Picador, 1992. A fascinating analysis of the cultural, philosophical and political boundaries that separate the individual from society.

The Global 2000 Report to the President by Gerald O. Barney, published by Viking, 1982. A look at the alarming trends in species and habitat loss, and increased desertification that science revealed during the 1970s.

Changing Consciousness by David Bohm and Mark Edwards, published by Harper Collins, 1991. Theoretical physicist Bohm and photographer Edwards present a dialogue about the vicious cycle of our thought processes and the disharmony between intellect and emotions alongside a direct, visceral photo essay on modern crises.

Eco-Economy: Building an Economy for the Earth by Lester R. Brown, published by Norton, 2001. The founding director of the Earth Policy Institute appeals for harmony between economic activity and natural resources.

Plan B: Rescuing a Planet Under Stress and a Civilization in Trouble by Lester R. Brown, published by Norton, 2003. A direct plea to the US leadership to take a lead in refocusing resources from military power to sustainable global economics.

Silent Spring by Rachel Carson, published by Houghton Mifflin, 1962. The first, crushing account of ecological degradation and agricultural poisons and pollutants in the food chain, widely credited with bringing environmental issues into the mainstream.

The New Economy of Nature: The Quest to Make Conservation Profitable by Gretchen Daily and Katherine Ellison, published by Island Press, 2002. A richly informative account of the dynamic interplay between science, economics, business and politics that will be required to create lasting models for conservation.

Collapse: How Societies Choose to Fail or Survive by Jared Diamond, published by Allen Lane, 2005. An investigation into how past civilizations became extinct because of their failure to recognize the limits of their natural resources and the power of nature.

One with Nineveh: Politics, Consumption and the Human Future by Paul R. and Anne H. Ehrlich, published by Island Press, 2004. A sweeping study of current environmental trends, and an urgent call for radical politics and individual action to prevent impending disaster.

Earthrise by Herbert Girardet, published by Paladin, 1992. How to turn the tide against environmental catastrophe.

No-Nonsense Guide to Climate Change by Dinyar Godrej, published by Verso/New Internationalist, 2001. Sifts scientific theory from scientific fact and presents the impacts on health, farming and wildlife, along with an analysis of political negotiations on the issue and potential solutions to it.

Refashioning Nature by David Goodman and Michael Redclift, published by Routledge, 1991. Subtitled *Food, Ecology and Culture*, this book shows how the production and consumption of food influences global development and interdependence.

Earth in the Balance by Al Gore, published by Houghton Mifflin, 1992. Published in the year he was elected vice-president of the USA, Gore was the first politician of his stature to tie his colours to the mast of the environmental cause.

The Third Revolution by Paul Harrison, published by I.B. Tauris in association with Penguin Books, 1992. How population growth, rising consumption and damaging technologies have combined to create the biggest environmental crisis in human history

Natural Capitalism by Paul Hawken, Amory Lovins and L. Hunter Lovins, published by Little, Brown, 1999. How cutting-edge companies are adopting practices that are more efficient and profitable while also saving the environment and creating jobs, presenting a template for a more sustainable future.

The Ending of Time by J. Krishnamurti and David Bohm, published by Victor Gollancz, 1985. This discussion between a leading religious teacher and an eminent physicist asks the question: "Has humanity taken a wrong turn that has brought about endless division, conflict and destruction?"

Freedom from the Known by J. Krishnamurti, edited by Mary Lutyens, published by Victor Gollancz, 1969. A selection of Krishnamurti's talks.

All the Marvelous Earth by J. Krishnamurti, published by Krishnamurti Publications of America, 2000. A selection of writings, published posthumously, on nature and human nature, illustrated with pictures chosen by Mark Edwards and Evelyne Blau.

Facing a World in Crisis by J. Krishnamurti, published by Shambhala Publications, 2005. A selection of talks that Krishnamurti gave on how to live in and respond to troubling and uncertain times. His message of personal responsibility and the importance of connecting with the broader world is presented in a non-sectarian and non-political way.

On Nature and the Environment by J. Krishnamurti, published by Victor Gollancz, 1992. The first volume in a series of thematic selections from Krishnamurti's works, it explains how the inner world of thoughts and emotions is linked to the outer world of humanity and environment.

The Sixth Extinction: Patterns of Life and the Future of Humankind by Richard E. Leakey and Roger Lewin, published by Doubleday, 1995. Paleoanthropologist Leakey and evolutionary scientist Lewin argue for a drastic reduction in our environmental impacts, to prevent species extinction through overcultivation and habitat destruction.

The Carbon War: Dispatches from the End of the Oil Century by Jeremy Leggett, published by Allen Lane, 1999. A sobering history of the oil industry and global-warming primer by oil-entrepreneur-turned-Greenpeace-scientist Leggett, founder of the UK-based renewable energy pioneers Solar Century.

Half Gone: Oil, Gas, Hot Air and the Global Energy Crisis by Jeremy Leggett, published by Portobello Books, 2005. How our addiction to carbon-based fuels threatens to drag us towards economic and environmental catastrophe.

Global Environmental Challenges of the Twenty-First Century by David Lorey (ed.), published by Scholarly Resources, 2002. A thought-provoking compilation of essays and articles on the environmental problems that threaten all life on our planet, and how they can be addressed.

Gaia: A New Look at Life on Earth by James Lovelock, published by Oxford University Press, 1979. A classic look at the earth as a living, self-regulating organism.

The Revenge of Gaia: Why the Earth Is Fighting Back – and How We Can Still Save Humanity by James Lovelock, published by Allen Lane, 2006. Lovelock's latest update on the state of the planet controversially advocates the adoption of nuclear energy to help lessen our impact on the earth's natural systems.

High Tide: News from a Warming World by Mark Lynas, published by Flamingo, 2004. The human cost of climate change, viewed by Lynas as he travels around the world.

The End of Nature by Bill McKibben, revised edition published by Bloomsbury, 2003. A groundbreaking plea for radical and life-renewing change. The author argues that for the world to survive, we must make a fundamental philosophical shift in the way we relate to nature.

Radical Ecology: The Search for a Liveable World by Carolyn Merchant, published by Routledge, 1992. The major philosophical, ethical, scientific and economic roots of environmental problems and how radical ecologists can transform science and society in order to sustain life.

Amazon Watershed by George Monbiot, published by Michael Joseph, 1991. An exploration of the underlying reasons for deforestation in the Amazon and why efforts to prevent it are so unsuccessful.

Ecology, Community and Lifestyle: Outline of an Ecosophy by Arne Naess, translated by David Rothenberg, published by Cambridge University Press, 1990. A revised and expanded translation of Naess' book *Okologi, Samfunn og Livsstil*, which sets out the author's thinking on the relevance of philosophy to the problems of environmental degradation and the rethinking of the relationship between mankind and nature.

Shadow Cities: A Billion Squatters, a New Urban World by Robert Neuwirth, published by Routledge, 2004. A history of squatting and property rights, from the settling of America to the teeming slums of modern Rio, Delhi, Istanbul, Nairobi and other cities where the dispossessed offer a preview of the world's urban future.

The World According to Pimm: A Scientist Audits the Earth by Stuart Pimm, published by McGraw-Hill, 2001. A witty and forceful assessment of our "global biological accounts", and a call for the worldwide adoption of ecological best practice.

A Green History of the World by Clive Ponting, published by Sinclair-Stevenson, 1991. Cutting through the superficial notions of progress, this pioneering study provides a picture of how modern societies emerged from prehistoric groups of hunter-gatherers.

Capitalism As If the World Matters by Jonathon Porritt, published by Earthscan Publications, 2005. The co-founder of Forum for the Future delivers a politically charged analysis of how capitalism can be modified to provide a future of wealth, equity and ecological integrity.

Toxic Sludge is Good for You!: Lies, Damn Lies and the Public Relations Industry by Sheldon Rampton and John Stauber, published by Common Courage Press, 1995. A coruscating account of PR double-speak on behalf of environmentally irresponsible corporations and other areas of business and government.

The Voice of the Earth by Theodore Roszak, published by Bantam Press, 1993. This exploration of ecopsychology from the author of *Counterculture in the 1960s* aims to expose the human roots of today's ecological crisis.

Red Sky at Morning: America and the Crisis of the Global Environment by James Gustave Speth, published by Yale University Press, 2004. The dean of the Yale School of Forestry and Environmental Studies sounds the alarm on the seriousness of the global environmental crisis. The failure, for which he says the US must take much of the blame, stems from a focus on the symptoms rather than on the underlying causes of environmental degradation, such as population size, affluence and technology.

Africa in Crisis: The Causes and Cures of Environmental Bankruptcy by Lloyd Timberlake, published by Earthscan, 1985. A rigorous examination of environmental catastrophe and agricultural collapse across Africa, showing how a revival in farming can help underpin economic development.

Only One Earth by Barbara Ward and René Dubois, published by André Deutsch, 1972. An unofficial report commissioned by the United Nations in time for the UN conference on the human environment, it was prepared with the assistance of a 152-member committee of consultants in 58 countries.

The Future of Life by Edward O. Wilson, published by Knopf, 2002. Pulitzer Prize-winning naturalist Wilson's impassioned and brilliantly argued manifesto for global conservation "to save the integrity of this planet and the magnificent life it harbors".

Our Common Future by the World Commission on Environment and Development, published by OUP, 1987. The full text of The Brundtland Report, the document that launched the concept of sustainable development into the political arena, advocating an economic model that does not harm, and at best can enhance the environment.

Journals

American Scientist www.americanscientist.org
Boston Globe www.boston.com
Christian Science Monitor www.csmonitor.com
Ecologist www.theecologist.org
Geographical www.geographical.co.uk
Green Futures www.greenfutures.org.uk
Guardian www.guardian.co.uk
Independent www.independent.co.uk
Los Angeles Times www.latimes.com
Mother Jones www.motherjones.com
National Geographic www.nationalgeographic.com
Nature www.nature.com
New Internationalist www.newint.org
The New Republic www.tnr.com
New Scientist www.newscientist.com
New York Times www.nytimes.com
New York Review of Books www.nybooks.com
Observer www.observer.guardian.co.uk
Resurgence www.resurgence.org
Scientific American www.sciam.com
Utne Reader www.utne.com
Washington Post www.washingtonpost.com

We would welcome information about other relevant books, journals and sites, so we can update future editions of this book and our website www.hardrainproject.com

Acknowledgements

I owe a lot more than thanks to the Tuareg nomad who rescued me, and to Bob Dylan who gave permission to publish "A Hard Rain 's A-Gonna Fall".

I am deeply indebted to the late J. Krishnamurti, who stands alone in his acute powers of perception and sensitivity to the natural world and to human nature, and to Professor David Bohm. Krishnamurti and Bohm wrote a number of books together and shared a passionate interest in exploring the deeper causes of our problems. They looked at the state of the world as a first step to examining the way each of us lives his or her life. They ask what kind of mind is capable of responding to events in the world and explore the physiological origins of our collective problems in our own personal lives and relationships. They invite the reader to see if a radically new worldwide approach might emerge from such an exploration. Their books are highly recommended.

I am grateful to David Skitt for permission to quote from his superb introduction to *Facing a World in Crisis*, and for the many memorable and very enjoyable conversations we have had, usually in Soho restaurants.

I haven't (knowingly) quoted from *Understanding the Present* by Brian Appleyard but it made a deep impression on me when I read it some years ago. Its echoes can be felt in "World Gone Wrong".

Occasionally reviews give such a complete account of a book that you feel you barely need to read it. This was the case with Clifford Geertz's review of Jared Diamond's latest book *Collapse: How Societies Choose to Fail or Survive*, which appeared in the *New York Review of Books*, March 24, 2005. I will read the book, but for the moment have drawn on Diamond's ideas via Geertz. I took the *King Lear* quote in paragraph 26 from a fascinating article by Bill Moyers, "Welcome to Doomsday", in the same issue of the magazine. Thanks to you all.

The UK media have covered poverty, environmental and human rights issues in great depth and detail, but a special debt is owed to Michael McCarthy of the *Independent*, Geoffrey Lean of the *Independent on Sunday*, John Vidal, editor of the *Guardian*'s environment page, the prolific Fred Pearce, whose illuminating contributions to *New Scientist* go back a long way, and to the front-row activist and writer George Monbiot.

I lifted the last sentence of paragraph 6 from *National Geographic Magazine*, "The Case of the Missing Carbon", February 2004. I also borrowed part of paragraphs 15 and 20 from Comment and Analysis in the *Independent on Sunday*, June 12, 2005. The quote by Bob Dylan in paragraph 6 is from an interview with Robert Hilburn in *Mojo*, September 2005, and the quotes in paragraph 28 are from *Dylan: Behind the Shades* by Clinton Heylin, published by Penguin Books.

Thanks to all my friends who helped as this book took shape, and especially to Chris Steele-Perkins, Jocelyn Bain Hogg, Steve Jackson, Philippe Achache, Hjalte Tin, Ali Paczensky, Alexander Finger, Ida Klemann, Mark Carwardine, Dexter Lane, Martin Batt, Kenny Young, Tom Burke and Herbie Girardet. I owe a special debt of gratitude to Theresa de Salis and the superhuman crew at Still Pictures. Without them this book could not have been attempted. I am very grateful to Tim Smit and the uniquely creative team at the Eden Project – Jo Readman, Sue Hill, Mike Petty and David Craddock. They gave support while this project found its feet and provided just the right blend of criticism, advice and encouragement.

Hard Rain has been a team effort. I was fortunate that Lloyd Timberlake wrote "No Shelter" for this book. It makes for a hard read but there's nothing hidden between the lines. Lloyd is uniquely qualified to write this essay – you'll find thousands of entries under his name on Google but you won't find out that he juggled with Dylan at Earl's Court during the Never Ending Tour. It's a lovely story and it's a pity this isn't the place to tell it.

I have been lucky to have worked with Mike Kenny on many projects. His patience is legendary and was tested to the full as *Hard Rain* evolved through many versions. I am most grateful to Mark Reynolds for his contribution to this project. No call or email went unanswered. His commitment became something I could not do without.

Many thanks to Charlie Jacoby, who cheerfully took on the task of compiling the web list for "What'll You Do Now?", and to Kristina Blagojevitch who proofread all our contributions.

Finally I want to express special thanks to Dan Bushell and Gary Bhupsingh of Sony/ATV Publishing (UK) Ltd and to Jeff Rosen at Easy Rider Music. Without their help this book would not have been published.

Mark Edwards

Still Pictures Moving Words is a new publishing venture springing from Mark Edwards' Still Pictures photo agency. *Hard Rain* is the first in a series of hard-hitting illustrated books exploring the issues that will define the 21st century. As a company, and as a network of like-minded individuals, we are committed to sustainable business operations, from using green electricity to minimizing heat loss and energy usage and recycling waste.

We have offset the residual carbon footprint of this book's production by purchasing land on behalf of the Gurukula Botanical Sanctuary in Kerala, India, set aside for the planting of trees, the conservation of native flora and fauna, and the restoration of degraded habitats. We'll post pictures and progress reports at hardrainproject.com.

This book was printed by Beacon Press using their *pure***print**® environmental print technology, which minimizes the negative environmental impacts of the printing process. Vegetable-based inks were used throughout, and 85% of the dry waste and 95% of the cleaning solvents associated with this production were recycled. Beacon Press uses 100% renewable energy, is a CarbonNeutral® company, has ISO 14001 and EMAS environmental assurance accreditation, and holds the Queen's Award for Enterprise: Sustainable Development.

The book is printed on McNaughton Era Silk, a recycled paper containing 50% post-consumer waste and 50% virgin fibre from sustainable forests, bleached using elementally chlorine-free processes. The cover is laminated with *purelam* biodegradable lamination.

A donation of 50p from every sale of this book is pledged to the Eden Project's Education Centre, The Core, to help fund its ongoing exhibitions, workshops/classes and Public Talkshops.

For more information on the issues raised in this book, visit
www.hardrainproject.com

For information about future titles, visit
www.stillpicturesmovingwords.com

"You cannot solve the problem with the same kind of thinking that has created the problem."

Albert Einstein